Original title:

Habit Makeover

Author: Clement Portlander

ISBN HARDBACK: 978-9916-88-310-5

ISBN PAPERBACK: 978-9916-88-311-2

Rising from the Old

From ashes gray, new dreams arise,
Old tales whispered in the skies.
With roots deep in the earth's embrace,
We find our strength, our rightful place.

The past may fade, yet it remains,
In every joy and all the pains.
Together we weave the threads of time,
Creating hope in every rhyme.

Reshaping the Familiar

Familiar paths twist and bend,
Like rivers flowing, they transcend.
With eyes anew, we see the signs,
Life's canvas shifts; the art defines.

Ancient echoes call our name,
In these spaces, we're not the same.
We paint with colors bold and bright,
Transforming shadows into light.

Embracing New Horizons

Beneath vast skies, we spread our wings,
A journey starts, oh how it sings!
With every step, the world expands,
Adventure waits in distant lands.

The horizon calls with promises sweet,
New tales await with every heartbeat.
We'll chase the sun, explore the night,
In every moment, we find ouright.

Crafting Fresh Rituals

In quiet moments, we create,
New traditions that celebrate.
With laughter shared and stories spun,
Together, we become as one.

Each gesture holds a sacred space,
A dance of joy, a warm embrace.
With open hearts and hopeful minds,
In these fresh rituals, love binds.

A Journey in Small Shifts

Each step we take, small and slight,
Guiding us softly, through day and night.
With whispers of hope, the path unfolds,
In gentle waves, our story told.

Mountains of doubt, we climb with care,
Finding new strength, in the open air.
The world may tremble, yet we stand tall,
In small steps forward, we conquer all.

Seeds of Change Sprout

From tiny seeds, great dreams arise,
Beneath the soil, beneath the skies.
With patient hands, we tend the ground,
In silent hope, new life is found.

Each raindrop falls, a whispered prayer,
Nurturing wishes, spreading everywhere.
Roots intertwine, with strength and grace,
In the garden of change, we find our place.

Transformative Moments

In fleeting seconds, life can shift,
A spark ignites, an unknown gift.
With open hearts, we greet the dawn,
New paths emerge, as old ones yawn.

Embrace the change, let fear take flight,
In transformative moments, we find our light.
With courage held, we face the day,
In every heartbeat, we learn to sway.

Navigating New Currents

The river flows with unseen force,
Guiding our spirits along their course.
With courage found in each new bend,
We sail through waters, we learn to mend.

Though storms may rise, and tides may turn,
In every struggle, there's much to learn.
We chart our paths with hope in sight,
Navigating currents, toward the light.

The Dawn of New Patterns

In morning's glow, hopes arise,
With colors bright, we touch the skies.
Each moment fresh, a canvas wide,
Embrace the change, let dreams collide.

The whispers of the dawn unfold,
New stories waiting to be told.
As sun ignites the world anew,
We dance in light, our spirits true.

Shifting Shadows of Routine

In corners dim where shadows play,
Routine grips tight, it's hard to sway.
Yet in the gloom, a spark may flare,
To break the bonds, to shift the air.

The clock ticks on, but hearts may roam,
In search of paths that lead us home.
With every step, we redefine,
The patterns forged, no longer mine.

Threads of Change We Weave

With every thread, a story spun,
In tapestry, our lives are one.
Colors blend, and patterns grow,
In gentle hands, the feelings flow.

Each twist and turn, a choice we make,
In fragile seams, the dreams awake.
The fabric of our days unfolds,
In vibrant hues, a life retold.

Breaking the Chains of Monotony

These chains that bind, they weigh us down,
In silent screams, we wear a frown.
But in our hearts, a fire stirs,
To break these bounds, we send our spurs.

With every day, a chance to fight,
To claim the spark, to seek the light.
The prison fades, and freedom sings,
As we take flight on daring wings.

Turning Over a Leaf

In the hush of autumn's grace,
Leaves fall gently, a soft embrace.
Every hue, a story told,
Whispers of change, brave and bold.

New paths emerge underfoot,
With each step, old roots we cut.
Renewed spirit in the breeze,
A dance of time among the trees.

In the cycle, life unfolds,
Lessons etched in shades of gold.
Turning over, fresh and bright,
We welcome dawn, embracing light.

The Mosaic of Reinvention

Fragments lost, now found anew,
A kaleidoscope in every view.
Peaceful chaos we create,
Intricate patterns to contemplate.

Shadows blend with brilliant light,
Old and new in constant flight.
Each piece speaks of journeys vast,
A tapestry, both bold and vast.

Voices merge in a symphony,
From discord springs sweet harmony.
In unity, we redefine,
The beauty of a changing line.

Paving the Way to Renewal

With each stone laid, purpose found,
Paths to freedom, safe and sound.
Brick by brick, our dreams take shape,
Hopeful hearts, we drape and drape.

The journey long, yet oh so sweet,
With every turn, we feel the beat.
Nature guides with gentle hand,
Leading us to promised land.

In resilience, we find our way,
Each stumble, a chance to sway.
Together rising, standing tall,
In the light, we'll never fall.

The Alchemy of Repetition

In cycles spun, old rhymes ignite,
Transforming shadows into light.
The heartbeat of a steady beat,
Whispers woven in rhythms sweet.

From the ashes, we renew,
Every echo, a different view.
Crafting change with tender care,
In each moment, love laid bare.

Through the lens of tried and true,
We discover paths anew.
Alchemy sings in the air,
Repetition, magic everywhere.

Winds of Change

The winds whisper tales anew,
Of paths unworn, and visions true.
They sweep away the dust of time,
And beckon hearts to seek the climb.

With every gust, the old must bow,
Embracing now, the sacred vow.
For seasons shift, and leaves must turn,
In vibrant hues, we start to learn.

Through valleys low and mountains high,
The winds will sing, the spirits fly.
A journey born of life's embrace,
In every heart, we find our place.

So let the winds of change arise,
With open arms, we touch the skies.
With every breath, we dare to dream,
In unity, we find our stream.

Turning the Pages of Routine

Each dawn arrives with borrowed light,
In gentle hues, it bids goodnight.
Yet in the rhythm, still we find,
A spark of courage, unconfined.

With every tick, the clock's refrain,
A call to dance, to break the chain.
We turn the pages, seek the new,
In simple acts, our spirits grew.

The humdrum fades, we chase the thrill,
In whispered dreams, we find the will.
A brand new chapter waits afar,
Our hearts ignite, we soar like stars.

Routine may weave its steady thread,
Yet we can leap where few have tread.
Each page a step, a chance to play,
In life's grand book, we find our way.

The Engine of Evolution

In shadows deep, ideas spark,
A flicker bright against the dark.
Innovation whispers in the night,
Unfolding visions, taking flight.

The gears of change begin to spin,
A dance of progress, deep within.
With every turn, the future calls,
The engine roars, as old life falls.

With patience forged in trial and tear,
We rise anew, and shed our fear.
Each step a note in nature's song,
A symphony where we belong.

So let the engine churn and grind,
With hearts aligned, we'll seek and find.
Through trial, error, and belief,
We craft the world beyond our grief.

Layers of Renewal

Like petals shed, we start again,
In every loss, a whispered gain.
The layers wrap, a tale so bold,
In stories shared, our hearts unfold.

Beneath the earth, the roots will dive,
In silence deep, we learn to thrive.
As seasons shift, we paint the skies,
In shades of hope, our spirits rise.

With each new dawn, we shed the past,
A dance of change, so fierce, so vast.
We find the strength in what we've missed,
In every layer, we exist.

So let the winds of change renew,
Each moment gold, each dream so true.
In layers joined, we rise above,
In every heart, we learn to love.

Imprints of Possibility

Footprints on the shore, so light,
Echoes of dreams that take flight.
Whispers of hope in the breeze,
Endless adventures waiting to seize.

Fingers trace paths in the sand,
Creating futures, bold and grand.
Each thought a brushstroke, so clear,
Painting a life without fear.

The horizon glows with the dawn,
As new beginnings are drawn.
Every heartbeat, a chance to explore,
Imprints of dreams that we adore.

The Canvas of Daily Rebirth

Each morning unfurls like a rose,
With colors that dance and compose.
Brushes of light paint the sky,
Echoing whispers of how to fly.

Every moment a fresh page turned,
With lessons and wisdom so earned.
Textures of laughter, shades of grace,
A vibrant life we embrace.

With strokes of kindness and joy,
Life's canvas we endlessly enjoy.
In each day's light we find our way,
Creating beauty, come what may.

Awakening Hidden Potential

Within each heart a seed lies deep,
Waiting for dreams to awake from sleep.
With water of courage and sunlight of hope,
We bloom and flourish, learn to cope.

Step by step, we rise through the haze,
Seeking the light of brighter days.
Unfolding layers, a fragrant new start,
Awakening the magic in every heart.

With whispers of strength and power,
We embrace our truth in every hour.
Endless potential, forever spread,
The journey continues, unafraid, we tread.

Shifting Sands of Routine

The clock ticks softly, marking time,
In patterns and rhythms, we often climb.
Yet within each moment, a chance to change,
To dance with the tides that feel so strange.

Familiar paths can feel so tight,
But shifting sands can bring new light.
Like waves that crash on the ocean's side,
We learn to embrace the shifting tide.

In every routine, a spark divine,
A call to adventure, a brand new line.
With hearts open wide, let's explore the unknown,
In shifting sands, our true selves are shown.

The Landscape of Transformation

Beyond the hills where daylight breaks,
New roads unfold, the past forsakes.
Each step reveals a hidden song,
In this landscape, we grow strong.

Branches bend with gentle grace,
Shadows dance in a warm embrace.
Nature whispers, softly calls,
Through every rise and every fall.

Mist and dew paint morning's light,
Colors shift from day to night.
We walk on paths both old and new,
In this journey, our spirits brew.

Hands entwined beneath the trees,
Carried forth on hopeful breeze.
Together we will build anew,
In this landscape, me and you.

Whispered Promises of Tomorrow

In twilight's glow, dreams take flight,
Whispers echo in the night.
Promises hang in the air,
Filling hearts with tender care.

Stars above, like distant friends,
Guide our hopes as daylight ends.
The moon smiles, a watchful eye,
Underneath its silver sky.

Each tomorrow blooms with grace,
Opening wide a vibrant space.
We step forth with faith so bright,
Chasing shadows, seeking light.

With every dawn, new stories weave,
Whispered promises we believe.
In the hush, our courage grows,
Grounded in love, as the world flows.

Renewed Paths

Upon the road where shadows tread,
New visions spark, old fears shed.
Every turn unveils a chance,
To dance along this wild expanse.

The earth beneath, a canvas wide,
Awaits our steps with arms open wide.
In the laughter of the trees,
We find strength within the breeze.

With each dawn, a fresh refrain,
Brightening thoughts, easing pain.
Paths unworn, they twist and glide,
In this journey, we will abide.

Through tangled woods, we forge ahead,
With every word, a bond is fed.
Together onward, hearts aligned,
In these renewed paths, love defined.

Transforming Shadows

Underneath the starlit dome,
Shadows stretch, they start to roam.
Flickering light reveals the past,
But in the dark, our hopes are cast.

Whispers linger, secrets shared,
In every shadow, dreams are bared.
A dance of light and dark entwined,
In this journey, hearts aligned.

Transformation sings a song,
In shadows where we once belonged.
Each step forward, a shift in view,
Darkness morphs to something new.

Together facing the unknown,
In transforming shadows, we have grown.
Embrace the night with open arms,
For in this realm, we find our charms.

The Beauty of Experimentation

In the quiet of the mind, ideas take flight,
Curiosity dances through the canvas of night.
With each brushstroke, a world to explore,
Uncharted paths lead to wisdom's core.

Sometimes we stumble, sometimes we soar,
Mistakes become treasures, opening doors.
Each failure a lesson, a step on the way,
To a brighter tomorrow, where dreams come to play.

Embrace every moment, the high and the low,
Life's richest colors emerge from the flow.
With courage and laughter, the heart learns to sing,
In the beauty of trying, we find our own wings.

So let us create, let our spirits ignite,
In the beauty of experimentation, we find our own light.

Portraits of Daily Transformation

Morning whispers secrets, with each gentle rise,
A moment to pause, to open our eyes.
The sun spills its gold on the street and the trees,
Transforming the mundane, like a soft summer breeze.

In small acts of kindness, a life can renew,
With laughter and love, we craft our debut.
Each evening's reflection, a mirror within,
The portrait of growth where we truly begin.

Seasons may shift, yet we stand with grace,
In the dance of existence, we find our own space.
Each challenge embraced becomes part of our song,
In the richness of change, we all can belong.

So sketch out your story, let it evolve,
In the portraits of daily, our mysteries solve.

Color in the Everyday

A splash of bright red in the morning's embrace,
The splash of a puddle as children all race.
Golden hues of laughter fill the air with delight,
Painting our moments with colors so bright.

A quiet cup of coffee, the aroma so sweet,
The soft rustle of leaves beneath eager feet.
Each fleeting encounter, a brush stroke divine,
In the mural of life, our hearts intertwine.

In the rhythm of footsteps on bustling streets,
Patterns emerge in the lives that we meet.
Each color a story, a thread finely spun,
Weaving through shadows, until day is done.

So cherish the moments, the vivid display,
For color in the everyday lights up the way.

The Personal Renaissance

In the heart's quiet chamber, old dreams reignite,
A spark in the dark, a flicker of light.
With courage we venture to craft a new scene,
In the tapestry woven, to be bold and serene.

We shed old skins, like leaves in the fall,
Emerging anew from the shadows that call.
Each moment a canvas, fresh thoughts to bestow,
In the personal renaissance, we learn to let go.

From the ashes of doubt, we rise with a song,
With brushes of passion, where we all belong.
Each color a heartbeat, each stroke a sweet prayer,
In the dance of rebirth, we discover our care.

So step into the light, let your spirit take flight,
In the personal renaissance, we find our own might.

A Chronicle of Fresh Starts

In the morning's gentle light,
We rise to meet the dawn.
Each breath a brand new chance,
A canvas to be drawn.

With every step we take,
The past begins to fade.
We build our dreams afresh,
In hopes that we have laid.

The whispers of our hearts,
Guide us on this path.
Through struggles and through joys,
We find our very wrath.

So let us forge ahead,
With courage in our hands.
For every fresh start made,
A life that understands.

Sprouting New Paths

Seeds planted in the earth,
Await the sun's warm kiss.
From darkness into light,
They stretch for hope and bliss.

With careful tending hands,
We guide their growth each day.
New paths begin to form,
In vibrant shades of gray.

Through rain and gentle winds,
They sway with strength anew.
In unison they rise,
To claim their place in view.

The world is full of green,
Where dreams take root and thrive.
In every sprouting heart,
A pulse that feels alive.

Flickers of Aspiration

In the quiet of the night,
A spark begins to glow.
Dreams dance like fireflies,
In whispers soft and low.

With every thought we weave,
A tapestry takes flight.
The flickers of our hopes,
Illuminate the night.

We rise to chase the stars,
With courage as our guide.
Each flicker fuels our fire,
To stand and not to hide.

For in our hearts we know,
That aspirations bloom.
We'll weave our own bright fate,
And banish all the gloom.

Cores of Reinvention

In the depths of our souls,
Lie whispers of the new.
We delve into our cores,
And find a strength that's true.

With every choice we make,
We shed the worn-out cloak.
Reinvention calls our name,
With every word we spoke.

Layers peel away slow,
To find the heart inside.
A journey rich with growth,
Where fears can no longer bide.

Embrace the change within,
With open arms we leap.
For in our core's embrace,
New dreams awaken deep.

A Symphony of Fresh Decisions

In the dawn's gentle light,
New choices take flight,
With courage, we move on,
Awakening the dawn.

Whispers of change in the air,
Our hearts are laid bare,
Each step a new song,
To where we belong.

Trust in the rhythm's flow,
Letting old worries go,
With every note, we find,
A melody of the mind.

Embrace the sweet unknown,
In this symphony grown,
Together we will soar,
To the open door.

The Art of Redesigning Days

Canvas of each new morn,
Colors bright and worn,
Sketching dreams anew,
With a vibrant hue.

Pastels blend with bold strokes,
Life's palette invokes,
A brush of joy and pain,
Every day we gain.

Lines may curve and twist,
Yet, there's beauty missed,
In imperfections seen,
Crafting what might be.

So, let the paint pour free,
In moments we truly see,
The art of living bright,
Designing pure delight.

Rethinking the Everyday Canvas

A canvas stretched so wide,
With each moment, we bide,
Stains of laughter and tears,
Reflecting all our years.

Every stroke tells a tale,
In colors that prevail,
Reimagining the scene,
In spaces yet unseen.

Details tiny but grand,
Life's brush in our hand,
A fresh take on the norm,
In the mundane, we transform.

So, let's paint with grace,
Finding joy in this place,
Rethink the shades of gray,
In the art of our day.

Transforming Echoes of Yesterday

Echoes soft yet clear,
Whispering what we fear,
Lessons from the past,
In memories, we're cast.

Shadows linger close by,
Yet, we learn to fly,
Transforming what has been,
Into hope to glean.

Through the veil of the night,
We find our own light,
Turning echoes to song,
Where our hearts belong.

With each step we take,
Old echoes we remake,
In the dance of the now,
We honor, we allow.

Curves of Change

Life flows like a river, soft and wide,
Shifting paths where secrets abide.
Each twist and turn, a lesson learned,
In the heat of fire, the heart is burned.

Time dances lightly, a fleeting glance,
We sway with the seasons, embrace the chance.
In every change, a story unfolds,
Whispers of fate in the air, retold.

Beneath the starlit, midnight sky,
Dreams unfurl, and laughter flies.
Let the waves carve our way anew,
Curves of change, we journey through.

Together we walk, hand in hand,
Facing each curve, together we stand.
For in each shadow, light shall gleam,
Curves of change, a hopeful dream.

New Chords in Silent Spaces

In the hush where echoes play,
Strings awaken, night meets day.
Soft whispers float in the air,
New chords form from tender care.

Melodies rise, a sweet embrace,
In silent corners, find our place.
With each note, a breath of peace,
In stillness, chaos finds release.

Hearts in harmony, voices blend,
Notes like whispers, love to send.
In the quiet, a song is born,
New chords in silent spaces adorn.

Together we find that sacred ground,
In silent spaces, joy is found.
Through music's journey, side by side,
In new chords of love, we abide.

A Mode of New Existence

A dawn breaks softly, dreams take flight,
In a mode of new existence, find the light.
Colors bloom where shadows lay,
Amidst the noise, hear the sway.

Moments weave in a golden thread,
Whispers of hope, where we are led.
Each heartbeat sings a vibrant tune,
In the shadows, dance with the moon.

Paths once hidden now come clear,
In a mode of being, we draw near.
Embracing life with open hands,
A new existence, our heart commands.

Together we stand, strong and bright,
In this journey, hearts ignite.
For every end, a new start calls,
In a mode of existence, love enthralls.

Transitions of the Heart

In the stillness, seasons shift,
Gentle breezes carry the drift.
Tides pull at the strings we feel,
Transitions whisper, love is real.

Moments collide, then slowly part,
Navigating through the art.
With every change, a tale is spun,
Transitions of the heart have begun.

In the depths where courage grows,
Shadows dance, while hope still glows.
Each turn a chance to start again,
In the cycle where love can reign.

Together we navigate the dark,
In transitions, we find our spark.
With open hearts, we learn to see,
The beauty in every mystery.

Rebirth in the Morning Light

The dawn breaks soft and bright,
Whispers of hope take flight.
Birds sing in gentle cheer,
New beginnings drawing near.

The shadows of night retreat,
As golden rays we meet.
Each petal opens wide,
In this day, we take pride.

The world awakens anew,
With skies a clearer blue.
Promises dance on the breeze,
In morning's calm, we seize.

Embrace the warmth of day,
Let worries drift away.
In light, we find our way,
Rebirth in bright array.

The Alchemy of Daily Choices

Each moment, a chance to choose,
Paths we walk, the light we use.
With every thought and every deed,
We plant the thoughts and the seed.

A smile shared, a hand to lend,
These small acts can often mend.
In choices, power we find,
Transforming heart and mind.

The mundane turns to gold,
When hearts are brave and bold.
With honesty our guide,
In truth, we shall abide.

Through trials and every test,
We mold our paths, we do our best.
Each choice a thread in the weave,
In this life, we can believe.

Navigating the Currents of Change

Life's river flows and bends,
A journey with twists and ends.
With courage, we face the tide,
In the waves, we choose to ride.

Change can stir the deepest fears,
Yet also brings forth new gears.
With each shift, we learn to grow,
In the flux, our strength will show.

Let go of what cannot stay,
Embrace the here and now today.
The current leads us to new shores,
With open hearts, we'll find the doors.

In solitude or joyful throng,
We navigate where we belong.
With every lesson that we gain,
We learn to dance through the rain.

The Seeds of New Rituals

In quiet moments, seeds are sown,
Of rituals that we've outgrown.
We honor the past, then let it go,
Planting new ways for our hearts to grow.

A cup of tea, a book at hand,
Simple joys, a gentle stand.
With intention, we greet the day,
In every choice, our spirits play.

The rhythm of life we redefine,
With sacred acts, our souls align.
Connection deepens with each intent,
In mindfulness, our time is spent.

From morning light to evening's hush,
We weave our magic in a soft rush.
The seeds we plant will flourish bright,
In the garden of our heart, pure light.

Unraveled Routines

In the morning light we rise,
With coffee stirs and sleepy sighs.
Familiar paths begin to blur,
As whispers of the unknown stir.

The clock ticks soft, a gentle tease,
Of daily tasks and simple pleas.
Yet within the mundane day,
Lies a spark just waiting to play.

We pause to breathe, a moment's grace,
Letting stillness find its place.
Routine holds tight, but hearts want free,
To dance beyond what we can see.

Unraveled threads of comfort worn,
Craft new patterns, fresh and born.
Embrace the chaos, take a chance,
Life's a daring, lively dance.

Chasing New Directions

Starlit skies guide dreams anew,
As we wander paths less true.
With every step, a story grows,
In the wild where freedom flows.

Whispers of change call from afar,
Daring hearts to chase a star.
We follow trails that twist and wind,
Leaving the comfort zone behind.

In the journey, lessons bloom,
From shadows, light begins to loom.
Chasing visions, bold and bright,
Finding purpose in the night.

Each direction reveals a door,
Open it wide, there's so much more.
With courage kindled, we ignite,
New horizons in our sight.

The Art of Daily Change

Brush the dust off yesterday,
As morning light begins to play.
In small shifts, great worlds emerge,
Life's canvas waits, ready to purge.

A sip of tea, a change of tune,
Reveals the magic of the mundane rune.
Transform the routine, paint it bright,
With colors bold, a new insight.

Let the rhythm of life inspire,
In each stillness, set your fire.
Find beauty in the ebb and flow,
The art of change begins to grow.

From daily chaos, a poem spun,
In every heartbeat, we are one.
Embrace the unknown, dance and sway,
For change is life's eternal play.

Echoes of Altered Choices

In caverns deep where shadows lie,
Echoes linger, whispers sigh.
Choices made, like stones they cast,
Rippling waters of the past.

Each decision, a fork in time,
Creates a rhythm, a hidden rhyme.
The path unwinds, twisting fate,
With every turn, we contemplate.

Memories beckon, softly call,
Reminding us of the rise and fall.
In altered paths, we find our way,
The echo's song helps us stay.

These choices shape the lives we lead,
A melody in every deed.
Embrace the echoes, hear their voice,
For life unfolds with every choice.

Steps Beyond Yesterday

In the shadows of time, we tread,
Leaving footprints where dreams were led.
Each moment a whisper, soft and clear,
Steps leading forward, dismissing fear.

From the ashes of doubt, we rise,
With open hearts and hopeful eyes.
The past a lesson, not a chain,
We step into light, shedding pain.

With every path, a chance to grow,
To face the storms, and let love flow.
Beyond yesterday, futures sing,
In every heartbeat, new life springs.

Together we walk, hand in hand,
Building dreams in a vibrant land.
Steps beyond yesterday's embrace,
We find ourselves in this sacred space.

The Whirlwind of Change

In the stillness before the storm,
Change is brewing, new thoughts form.
A whirlwind stirs the settled sand,
Whispers of hope across the land.

Turning leaves under skies so wide,
We learn to dance with the turning tide.
Embrace the gusts, let go of fear,
For every ending brings life near.

Through the chaos, a chance unfolds,
Courage ignites as destiny molds.
In the heart of the tempest, find your way,
The whirlwind brings a brighter day.

With courage as our guiding star,
We'll journey far, no matter how bizarre.
In every swirl, a promise to grow,
The whirlwind of change teaches us so.

A Tapestry of New Choices

In threads of color, life we weave,
Every choice a pattern, a chance to believe.
Stitches of laughter, shadows of pain,
A tapestry rich, through loss and gain.

With each decision, a new design,
Paths intertwining, yours and mine.
We gather the strands, both bright and dull,
Creating a vision, beautifully full.

In choices made, we find our voice,
Crafting our lives, a personal choice.
Woven together, our stories align,
In this tapestry made, we truly shine.

Embrace the threads, both bold and shy,
For every piece tells a reason why.
A tapestry of new choices reflects,
The vibrant life that love connects.

Embrace the Unusual

In the corners where shadows creep,
Lie secrets and wonders, ours to keep.
Embrace the unusual, let go of the norm,
In quirks and oddities, new worlds form.

Amongst the chaos, a spark may ignite,
A dance of the strange brings colors to light.
In the unexpected, magic may dwell,
A whisper of stories too wild to tell.

With open minds, let's wander afar,
New paths unfold as we follow the bizarre.
In every odd twist, we find our song,
In the unusual, we truly belong.

So dance in the rain and play with the breeze,
Find joy in the unusual, live life with ease.
For in every peculiar, a treasure is found,
An embrace of the unusual spins wonders around.

Awakening to Possibilities

Stars fade softly into the night,
Whispers of dreams take flight.
Open hearts begin to see,
The path of hope calls out to be.

Colors dance in morning's glow,
Every moment starts to flow.
With each step, the world expands,
Endless futures in our hands.

Radical change can start today,
In every word we choose to say.
Casting fears into the breeze,
Awakening comes with ease.

Here we stand, with spirits bright,
Together fueling our own light.
Infinite chances wait in line,
Awakening to what is divine.

The Light of New Dawn

A new day breaks, the shadows flee,
Whispers of hope are wild and free.
Sunshine spills across the land,
Promises made, forever planned.

Mountains rise to greet the skies,
Where dreams are born, and courage lies.
With each heartbeat, fears dissolve,
In the light, we start to evolve.

Softly, the night gives way,
To vibrant hues of bright array.
Stories written in every ray,
The light of new dawn leads the way.

With open minds and open hearts,
A journey begins, as life imparts.
Every dawn, a chance to grow,
In the light, our spirits glow.

Disrupting the Monotony

Routine wraps around the day,
Familiar paths begin to fray.
Step outside the narrow lane,
Embrace the wild, break the chain.

Colors burst where none exist,
In the chaos, we find the bliss.
Jumps of joy, unchained and free,
Disrupt the dull, let it be.

Voices rise against the norm,
In new rhythms, we find our form.
Dance and sing, let laughter reign,
In breaking patterns, joy is gained.

With every twist, a spark ignites,
Imagination soars to new heights.
Disrupting all, find your own tune,
In the chaos, we are in bloom.

Crafting Tomorrow's Cadence

Hands come together, dreams ignite,
Every heartbeat takes its flight.
With vision clear, we carve the way,
Crafting tomorrow, starting today.

Echoes of laughter fill the air,
Crafted moments, treasures rare.
With each choice, we shape our fate,
In this symphony, love translates.

Melodies swirl through open space,
In the dance of time, we find our place.
Notes of courage, chords of light,
In crafting tomorrow, we unite.

Together we weave a vibrant song,
In a world where we all belong.
Armed with hope, let music play,
Crafting tomorrow's cadence today.

Beyond the Comfort Zone

In shadows of safe embrace,
We linger, we hesitate.
The echo of dreams once bright,
Calls softly, ignites the fight.

Step forward, the world awaits,
Where courage and heart create.
Beyond the walls we have known,
New paths and adventures shown.

Embrace the thrill of the unknown,
For seeds of growth are sown.
With every leap, we unfold,
Stories of bravery told.

So stretch your wings, take flight,
Let fear turn into light.
Beyond the comfort zone lies
A landscape where courage flies.

Awakened Intentions

In the quiet of dawn's glow,
Intentions begin to flow.
Whispers of dreams take form,
In this space, hearts grow warm.

With each breath, we declare,
The wishes we long to share.
Awakened, we stand renewed,
Ready to chase what ensued.

Clarity breaks through the haze,
Guiding us through life's maze.
With purpose, we rise and strive,
To nurture all that's alive.

So plant the seeds of your truth,
In the garden of your youth.
Awakened, we choose to be,
The architects of our destiny.

The Dance of Progress

In rhythm of steps we sway,
Progress unfolds day by day.
With each turn, a new embrace,
We find strength in the chase.

Twists of fate guide our move,
In every challenge, we groove.
Each stumble, a lesson learned,
Through effort, our passion burned.

The music plays, hearts align,
In this dance, our spirits shine.
Together we rise, never alone,
In strides of growth, we have grown.

So let the rhythm take flight,
In the darkness, we find light.
With open hearts, we advance,
In the beautiful dance of chance.

Shifting the Gear

As seasons change, so do we,
With every turn, we break free.
In the gears of life we turn,
New lessons in every yearn.

With a shift, we find our way,
To seize the promise of the day.
Adapting to what life bestows,
As the river of time flows.

In moments of pause, we reflect,
On choices made, the dreams we protect.
Change offers growth, a chance to ignite,
The passion within, a brilliant light.

So shift the gear, trust the ride,
With open hearts, we turn the tide.
In the dance of progress, we steer,
Towards a future that feels near.

Writing a Brighter Blueprint

With every stroke, a dream takes flight,
Plans unfold beneath the night.
A map of hopes we sketch with care,
In pursuit of futures bright and fair.

Each line a path, each word a guide,
We carve out life, with hearts open wide.
Daring visions, bold and true,
Writing a world built anew.

Awakening the Sleeping Self

In silence deep, where shadows lay,
A whisper calls, to light the way.
From slumber's grasp, we rise once more,
Awakening dreams we can't ignore.

The pulse of life begins to sing,
As we embrace the change it brings.
From cocooned hopes, we take our flight,
Reclaiming truths lost to the night.

Journeys into Uncharted Comforts

Beyond the shore, the legends dwell,
In waters blue, where stories swell.
We sail on winds of chance and fate,
To seek the calm that feels so great.

Each wave a tale, each breeze a friend,
In journeys vast that never end.
Discoveries made in distant lands,
Embrace the warm of new-found sands.

The Canvas of Courage

With brush in hand, we face the dawn,
On canvases where fears are drawn.
Each stroke a step, each hue a call,
To rise above, to never fall.

The colors clash, yet blend so bright,
A masterpiece born from the fight.
In every line, the heart we share,
The canvas blooms with bold flair.

Unfolding the Map of Possibility

In shadows deep, I find the light,
A path once closed, now bold and bright.
Each step I take, a choice to make,
Unlocking dreams, the world to take.

With ink and hope, the map expands,
A journey drawn by unseen hands.
Through valleys low and mountains high,
I chase the stars across the sky.

New roads appear as I explore,
With every turn, I crave for more.
The winding trails, they teach and guide,
In every twist, my heart's open wide.

In possibilities, I learn to sway,
Embracing change, come what may.
With courage found and spirits free,
I unfold the map; the world's for me.

A Dance with New Beginnings

With every dawn, a chance to twirl,
A melody in life unfurl.
Step by step, I find my place,
In rhythms soft, I learn to grace.

The music calls; my heart responds,
In every beat, a spirit bonds.
New paths invite the bold to start,
A dance ignites within the heart.

Each stumble turns to playful chance,
A twist of fate, a bright romance.
In every moment, joy abounds,
With leaps of faith, my spirit sounds.

As seasons shift and stories blend,
I find my strength, I transcend.
Together we shall dance and sing,
Embracing all that life can bring.

Embracing the Winds of Transition

The winds arise, they softly call,
Whispers guiding through it all.
As autumn leaves begin to fall,
I breathe in change, embracing all.

Each gust a chance to learn, to grow,
In every shift, I feel the glow.
The world transforms, so do I,
Like birds in flight, I learn to fly.

Through stormy skies and gentle rains,
I find the peace amidst the strains.
With every blow, I stand my ground,
In freedom's song, my spirit's found.

Embracing winds with open arms,
I dance with beauty, hold its charms.
This journey calls for hearts to soar,
In every breeze, I seek for more.

Chronicles of a Mind Reborn

In pages worn, the stories dwell,
Of trials faced, of battles fell.
Through sorrow's veil, a light breaks through,
In every chapter, strength anew.

The echoes of the past resound,
Yet wisdom gained is deeper found.
With every line, I weave my tale,
Of hopes revived and dreams set sail.

Through shadows cast, I rise once more,
A phoenix formed from ash before.
In mirrors clear, my truth reflects,
A mind transformed, no longer vexed.

The chronicles keep turning still,
With every breath, I find my will.
In stories told, I flourish, thrive,
A mind reborn, I'm so alive.

Crafting a Life Unscripted

With each step, I find my way,
Paths unwritten, come what may.
Dreams unfurling, wild and free,
A world of choices, just for me.

In the quiet, I hear the call,
To dance and stumble, to rise and fall.
Embracing moments, both big and small,
Crafting a life, where I stand tall.

Brush in hand, I paint my fate,
Colors swirling, I won't wait.
Each hue a story, vivid and bright,
A canvas of dreams, in morning light.

I'll weave my tale with threads of gold,
A tapestry of dreams, brave and bold.
Each stitch a memory, rich and rare,
Crafting a life beyond compare.

The Fire of Renewal

From ashes, sparks begin to rise,
A phoenix birthed beneath the skies.
The flames ignite a brand-new start,
With every ember, a hopeful heart.

Burning away the past we know,
In the heat of change, we learn and grow.
The fire cleanses, bright and rare,
Creating space for dreams laid bare.

A flicker dances, casting light,
Guiding us through the darkest night.
With every flame, a chance to mend,
In the fire of renewal, we transcend.

Let passion burn, let courage soar,
In the heat of life, we seek for more.
For in the blaze, we find our way,
To forge a brand new dawn each day.

Mosaic of Intentional Living

Pieces scattered, bright and bold,
In every moment, life unfolds.
With purpose woven in each seam,
A mosaic crafted from a dream.

Intentions guide each varied square,
Shaped by kindness, love, and care.
Together forming a vibrant scene,
The art of life, a balance keen.

Every fragment tells a tale,
Of joy and struggle, love prevails.
With each connection, hearts do sing,
In this mosaic, hope takes wing.

A tapestry of days gone by,
We build our world, aim for the sky.
With every piece, a chance to grow,
Living intentional, let love flow.

The Palette of Potential

Colors waiting, soft and bright,
In every soul, a spark of light.
From shades of doubt to hues of might,
A palette full, our hearts in sight.

With every brushstroke, dreams take flight,
Creating futures, pure delight.
The canvas beckons, wide and free,
Inviting all that we can be.

In vibrant shades of courage bold,
Tales of triumph, yet untold.
With each creation, bold we stand,
Embracing life with open hand.

Potential whispers, soft and clear,
It urges us to persevere.
And in this dance of brush and flair,
We paint our purpose, rich and rare.

Fractals of Newness

In patterns that twist and spin,
The dawn reveals what lies within.
A spark ignites the boundless skies,
Fractals dance before our eyes.

Each moment a chance to expand,
To traverse the uncharted land.
Triumphs born of dreams we chase,
In the weave of time and space.

Curves that twist, angles that bend,
Signaling change around the bend.
From chaos, order finds its way,
In fractals of newness, we sway.

With every breath, we redefine,
The edges of what is divine.
In a world of endless potential,
We journey through the quintessential.

Rhythm of the Uncustomary

In shadows where the unheard play,
A symphony in disarray.
Each note stirs a hidden thrill,
The heartbeat echoes, never still.

Unchained steps on pavements worn,
Movements light, yet never torn.
A dance that shatters the mundane,
Rhythm swells like summer rain.

Voices whisper, daring to change,
In silence, we find the strange.
The wild pulse of the unusual,
Crafting lives less habitual.

Between the lines of yesterday,
The uncustomary finds its way.
In every moment, bold and bright,
We chase the echoes of delight.

Breathing Life Into Tradition

With hands that mold the ancient clay,
Traditions twist in bright array.
We breathe in tales from the past,
Nurturing roots that hold us fast.

Old songs sung with vibrant flair,
Carrying love we choose to share.
In the tapestry of time's embrace,
We find our strength, our sacred place.

Like fire rekindled through the night,
We illuminate with shared light.
In every gesture, every song,
Tradition lives, where we belong.

To dance the steps of yore anew,
We honor paths that lead us true.
Each heartbeat whispers stories grand,
Breathing life into tradition's hand.

New Echoes in the Chamber of Days

In corridors where silence speaks,
Echoes linger, time streaks.
The past unveils its hidden grace,
New whispers fill this timeless space.

Each fleeting moment, a gift to take,
In the chamber where dreams awake.
A symphony of hopes reborn,
In shadows where the light is worn.

Through laughter's warmth and sorrow's plea,
New echoes blend in harmony.
Memories weave their vibrant thread,
In the tapestry of what's ahead.

As dawn unfolds, so does our song,
In the chamber where we belong.
With every heartbeat, strong and clear,
New echoes rise, forever near.

Patterns Rewoven

Threads of old, woven tight,
Colors blend, day and night.
Spinning tales of joy and strife,
In the loom, we weave our life.

Whispers soft, secrets shared,
With each knot, we show we cared.
Patterns shift, new ones arise,
In each twist, our spirit flies.

Echoes of the past resound,
With each turn, new paths are found.
In the fabric, stories bloom,
Crafting beauty from the gloom.

As we stitch, we mend what's torn,
From the ashes, dreams are born.
In the tapestry we create,
Life's emotions reverberate.

Breaking Old Molds

Fragments scatter, pieces fly,
Breaking free, we reach for the sky.
Old routines, they start to fade,
In the light, new plans are laid.

Chasing flaws that held us back,
Building strength, filling the crack.
Step by step, towards the light,
In the dawn, we find our might.

Fear and doubt, we cast them off,
With each heartbeat, we grow soft.
Breaking chains, embracing change,
In the wild, we feel so strange.

Molds once strong, now crumble down,
In the chaos, a brand new crown.
Revolution in every heart,
From the old, we craft new art.

The Rebirth of Schedule

Ticking clock, a silent guide,
Days unfold, like waves that glide.
Routine dances, fresh and bold,
In our hands, new tales are told.

Morning sun, a vibrant cheer,
Carving moments, crystal clear.
With each hour, we redefine,
In the passage, stars align.

Schedules bend, yet hold us tight,
In the rhythm, pure delight.
Tasks once weary now embrace,
In our lives, we find our space.

Evening whispers, time to rest,
In our dreams, we feel the quest.
Rebirth blooms with every dawn,
In the cycle, we are drawn.

A Canvas of New Beginnings

Brush in hand, can't hold it back,
Colors splash, fill every crack.
On this canvas, dreams are spun,
In every stroke, we become one.

Fresh horizons call our name,
In each hue, we fan the flame.
Blank spaces, ripe with desire,
In our hearts, we build a fire.

Lines may waver, shapes may blend,
In the chaos, rules we bend.
Art unfolds, like petals bloom,
In our hearts, we find the room.

Every splash, a story told,
In this life, we break the mold.
Canvas fresh, as we begin,
In the artwork, all is kin.

From Dusty Trails to Fresh Tracks

From dusty trails we start anew,
With each step, a world in view.
The path ahead, though worn and gray,
Leads us forth, come what may.

Whispers of dreams guide our way,
Through wildflowers in bright array.
We leave behind the shadows cast,
Embracing the moments, free at last.

With open hearts, we chase the light,
Through tangled woods, day turns to night.
Every footfall a promise made,
In this journey, we won't fade.

So here we stand where trails converge,
Facing the winds of change, we urge.
From dusty trails to fresh tracks drawn,
Together we'll rise with every dawn.

Steps Toward the Unfamiliar

Each step we take, a brave leap forth,
Into the realms of unknown worth.
With every heartbeat, fears subside,
We venture boldly, side by side.

The map unwritten, paths unclear,
Yet trust becomes our guiding steer.
In curiosity, we find our way,
Through the shadows, into the sway.

Voices of change call us near,
With every challenge, we shed the fear.
New horizons await our gaze,
In the dance of life, we'll find our grace.

Steps toward wonders yet unseen,
In every corner, magic gleams.
Together we'll stride, hand in hand,
Creating dreams in this vast land.

The Symphony of Choice

In life's grand hall, choices abound,
Each note we play, a melody found.
The strings of fate plucked with intent,
Crafting a song, our lives represent.

Harmony swells in the heart's refrain,
From whispered doubts to joyful gain.
Each decision like a beat in time,
A rhythm of hope in life's great rhyme.

Through discord and peace, we learn to flow,
Creating a symphony, high and low.
With courage, we choose the paths we take,
In this orchestra of life, we partake.

So listen close, the music plays,
In every choice, a new verse lays.
Together we compose our fate,
In the symphony of choice, we celebrate.

Fragments of Reformation

In shards of glass, the stories gleam,
Echoes of places where we dream.
From pieces broken, new forms arise,
Transforming pain into disguise.

Each fragment holds a tale untold,
Of battles fought and dreams of gold.
In the mosaic of hope, we find a way,
To weave our hearts through night and day.

With gentle hands, we shape and mend,
Turning the past into a friend.
Reformation springs from the cracks,
In the light, there are no lacks.

So let us gather all the hues,
In the beauty of change, we can choose.
Fragments of life, together we create,
A masterpiece of what awaits.

Finding Fresh Footprints

In the soft earth where shadows lay,
A trail emerges, guiding the way.
Each step whispers tales of old,
Of secrets waiting to be told.

The morning dew, a sparkling gem,
Beneath the trees, where wild things stem.
I tread lightly, with heart aglow,
Unraveling paths I long to know.

With every mark, a promise grows,
Of journeys found and love that flows.
In this dance between thought and time,
I find my peace, my silent rhyme.

So here I stand, amidst the light,
With fresh footprints, all feels right.
The world beckons, a soft embrace,
In finding footprints, I find my place.

A Sojourn in Change

Leaves turn gold in crisping air,
A fleeting moment, a breath to share.
Each season whispers, change must come,
In every ending, a new drum.

Paths once clear now twist and bend,
With each new turn, the rules suspend.
Embrace the shift of night to dawn,
In transformation, fears are gone.

Echoed laughter fills the skies,
As journeys shift and spirits rise.
With open hearts, we roam the trails,
In the realm of change, love prevails.

So take my hand, let's walk together,
In this sojourn, we'll brave the weather.
Though tides may turn and skies may gray,
With every change, we find our way.

A Symphony of New Voices

The morning breaks with songs anew,
Each voice a thread, a vibrant hue.
Together we weave a tapestry,
Of dreams and hopes, of harmony.

From distant hills, a choir rises,
Melodies wrapped in sweet surprises.
Unite the hearts, let music soar,
In every note, we crave for more.

The rhythm dances through the air,
With beats that spell a story rare.
In varied tones, we find our strength,
Through discord's trials, we go the length.

So gather 'round, let voices blend,
A symphony that will never end.
In every harmony, we'll rejoice,
For in our hearts, we have a choice.

The Voyage to Uncharted Practices

Set sails for lands unknown and wide,
With compass hearts, we'll turn the tide.
Each wave a promise, rich and deep,
Awakening dreams that lie in sleep.

The journey calls, the stars align,
In every storm, our fates entwine.
We seek the shores of new insight,
With courage fierce, we chase the light.

Uncharted waters, bold and free,
Reveal the depths of discovery.
Through trials faced and storms endured,
In every challenge, we'll be assured.

So follow me, through fog and dew,
To practices that feel so true.
In every voyage, we find our ground,
In uncharted ways, our hearts unbound.

Echoes of Intent

In shadows deep, where whispers roam,
A flicker glows, we call it home.
Intentions clear, like stars that shine,
Guiding hearts through space and time.

With every breath, our hopes take flight,
Chasing dreams into the night.
Echoes ring, our voices swell,
A symphony we weave so well.

Through laughter's joy and sorrow's pain,
We find the strength to rise again.
Each moment counts, a treasured gift,
In echoes, our spirits lift.

Together we stand, united as one,
Creating paths where all can run.
In the quiet, intents aligned,
Our futures bright, forever blind.

Building Bridges to Tomorrow

Across the rivers, wide and deep,
We seek the dreams that we must keep.
Hand in hand, we cross the night,
Building bridges, hearts in flight.

Each plank we lay, a tale unfolds,
Stories whispered, courage bold.
In unity, we find our voice,
Together, we shall make our choice.

The dawn will rise, with colors clear,
Transforming doubts into sincere.
With every step, foundations strong,
We build a world where all belong.

Through valleys low and peaks of light,
We'll forge the path to sacred sight.
On bridges high, we will not falter,
For tomorrow's dawn, we shall alter.

The Tapestry of Renewal

In threads of gold, we weave our days,
A tapestry that brightens ways.
Each stitch a story, rich and fine,
In moments shared, our lives entwine.

Through colors bright, we paint our lives,
In laughter's glow, our spirit thrives.
Renewal's dance, a vibrant flow,
A garden where our dreams can grow.

From ashes rise, new blooms shall greet,
In every heart, the pulse of beat.
Through trials faced, we find our grace,
In unity, we seek our place.

With open hands, we share our light,
Each thread a beacon, shining bright.
In the tapestry, hope's unfold,
A story of the brave and bold.

In Search of Playful Intent

In meadows wide, where laughter gleams,
We find the truth in playful dreams.
With open hearts, we chase the sun,
In every game, we're all as one.

Skipping stones on tranquil streams,
We dance in rhythm, lost in beams.
Each smile shared, a bond to seal,
In simple joy, our souls can heal.

Through winding paths and secret trails,
In the rustle of leaves, our spirit sails.
With childlike wonder, we explore,
In search of play, we crave for more.

Let's paint the sky with colors bright,
With playful intent, we take our flight.
In laughter's echo, we find release,
In our hearts, the joy of peace.

A Palette of New Patterns

Colors swirl in dazzling dance,
Each hue a chance for a fresh glance.
Brush strokes blend in radiant cheer,
Crafting visions that draw us near.

Textures whisper on canvas wide,
Embracing stories we cannot hide.
With every layer, we boldly create,
A masterpiece born of love and fate.

Shapes converge in symphonic flow,
Inviting hearts to rise and glow.
A palette rich with dreams untold,
In the art of life, let's be bold.

Witness beauty as it unfolds,
In the patterns that life beholds.
With each new stroke, we redefine,
A world anew, forever divine.

Reimagining the Daily Grind

Routine wraps like a well-worn cloak,
But beneath lies the spark of hope.
Shift perspectives, make time dance,
In mundane moments, find your stance.

Coffee brews in quiet morning,
Songs of birds, the day adorning.
Tasks await with a gentle nudge,
Embrace them all, refuse to budge.

Streets of sameness spark a thrill,
In every turn, a chance to fill.
With courage, face the well-trodden way,
Create new paths in the light of day.

Lift your eyes to the skies above,
In every breath, find space for love.
The everyday becomes alive,
With slight shifts, we thrive and strive.

Charting Unexplored Waters

Waves whisper secrets, deep and vast,
Inviting dreams from the past.
Set sail on ships of hope and grace,
In the sea of change, find your place.

Horizons beckon with a brand new song,
Across the tides where we belong.
Chart your course with steady hands,
Embrace the wonders life expands.

Stars above, like lanterns bright,
Guide us through the darkest night.
In uncharted realms, let courage grow,
Navigating paths we long to know.

With every wave, a story unfolds,
In the heart of the ocean, dreams are bold.
Together we forge through every storm,
In these waters, our spirits warm.

Tides of Transformation

Ebb and flow, the rhythms call,
Understanding life's great sprawl.
Each surge a chance to start anew,
As tides of change flow in and through.

Seas of struggle, shores of grace,
In every change, we find our place.
Wisdom flourishes as we release,
Old patterns fade, making space for peace.

With open hearts, we face the night,
Searching for that inner light.
Transforming pain into a song,
In unity, we all belong.

So rise with the dawn, embrace the day,
In tides of change, let's find our way.
Together we blossom, together we thrive,
In the dance of life, we truly arrive.

9 789916 883112